For

FATHERS
and
DAUGHTERS

That Special Relationship

Edited by
Barbara Kohn

PETER PAUPER PRESS, INC.
WHITE PLAINS, NEW YORK

*To my daughter, Laurie, who has gone
through all the stages in this book—
Daddy's Little Girl, Good Girl—Bad Girl,
Bride—and has become a beautiful
and self-assured young woman.*

With pride,
Mom

Copyright © 1994
Peter Pauper Press, Inc.
202 Mamaroneck Avenue
White Plains, NY 10601
All rights reserved
ISBN 0-88088-161-5
Printed in Hong Kong
7 6 5 4 3 2

CONTENTS

Introduction

Daddy is a daughter's first love, her hero, her protector and the person who makes her feel attractive and good about herself. It is through her father's eyes that a young girl first sees herself as other men might perceive her. Yet we assume that daughters are more influenced by their mothers, that they model themselves after their mothers. *Like mother, like daughter,* we say.

Recent studies about successful women and the secrets of their success indicate that, contrary to popular thought, fathers play a major role in their daughters' successes. The women studied integrated their fathers' values into their lives. Having loving, caring fathers who paid attention to them and were involved in their upbringing made the daughters feel that they could achieve anything they set out to do. When Hillary Rodham Clinton was told by her father, *I will always love you but I won't always like what you do,* he sent her a message that his unconditional love for her was not based on what she *did* but on who she was.

Conversely, women who do not have compassionate, loving fathers sometimes have problems dealing with the men in their personal and professional lives. These women expect to find in their husbands, partners, male colleagues and employers what was lacking in their fathers. Disappointed, they change men and jobs frequently.

*W*hat are fathers for? What do they provide that young women especially need and want? And why is the relationship between fathers and daughters so different from that between mothers and daughters? In this book some answers are offered by well-known psychiatrists and psychologists, political figures, writers, and celebrities. A common thread that runs through their comments is the need for a father's unconditional love and approval.

*A*s more fathers become caretakers and nurturers, and are no longer expected to be authority figures and sole providers, it is hoped that more daughters will become more secure in who they are. With self-assurance and pride they will say, *I am my father's daughter.*

B. K.

Daddy's Little Girl

✍ She is his adorable little girl, an angel, the apple of his eye.

✍ He is her first love, her hero, protector, provider.

$\mathcal{T}$he sons of God saw the daughters of men, that they were fair.

GENESIS 6:2

$\mathcal{I}$t is one a.m. and Katharine Haines Andersen, my first child, is already seven hours old... I had been told to expect all newborns to resemble Yoda or E. T., but with more wrinkles. But from the moment of her birth, with eyes open wide, she was a dark-haired, pink-cheeked beauty.

CHRISTOPHER ANDERSEN

$\mathcal{J}$eeves, I wish I had a daughter. I wonder what the procedure is?

Marriage is, I believe, considered the preliminary step, sir.

P. G. WODEHOUSE,
Carry On, Jeeves

[$\mathcal{P}$laying Mr. Mom was] hard work [and] lots of fun. Annie and I went everywhere and did everything together. I took her to business meetings—even real important ones. I'd be sitting there, and if some executive's phone rang a little too loud, I'd say, *Excuse me, but could you please lower your phone's ring? You're waking my daughter.* And if Annie needed care—if her diaper needed changing—the meeting came to a halt.

KEVIN COSTNER

*H*olding my wife Bonnie's hand in the delivery room while Erin was born didn't make me a mom. Caring for Erin every morning for sixteen months while my wife went back to work didn't make me a mom. Spending my days (I work nights) with my child while my wife worked made me a new-style father, perhaps. My dad certainly didn't do it. But my new-style father experiences did nothing to deactivate thirty-four years of training in being a man. Although I loved the role of father, that was always secondary in my mind to my ideal image of Mom.

DAVID BLASCO

9

When I was a little kid, a father was like the light in the refrigerator. Every house had one, but no one really knew what either of them did once the door was shut.

ERMA BOMBECK

I was not close to my father, but he was very special to me. Whenever I did something as a little girl—learn to swim or act in a school play, for instance—he was fabulous. There would be this certain look in his eyes. It made me feel great.

DIANE KEATON

She climbed into my lap and curled into the crook of my left arm. I couldn't move that arm, but I could cradle Ashtin in it. I could kiss the top of her head. And I could have no doubt that this was one of the sweetest moments of my life.

DENNIS BYRD,
about his daughter

Dad is what most sons call their fathers; *Daddy* is the term of endearment—even homage—of daughters.

FRANK PITTMAN

Fame is rot; daughters are the thing.

SIR JAMES BARRIE,
Dear Brutus

$\mathcal{M}$y daddy lived for his family. He loved me, cared for me, read me books, hugged me. I remember him driving up in his Volkswagen Beetle after his day in Washington and we would rush out of the house to greet him. We loved our Daddy. He always smelled so good. He always wore Old Spice, and to this day when I smell Old Spice, I remember hugging Daddy.

KATHIE LEE GIFFORD

$\mathcal{W}$hen my daughter says to her father, *Oh, Daddy, I like your tie,* she seems to imply by tone and manner that he nurtured the worms, harvested the silk, designed the pattern, sewed in the lining and invented the four-in-hand knot, all before breakfast.

ANNA QUINDLEN

$\mathcal{T}$his year you'll see the face not of the comic and the fool, but a man who at age 66 received one of God's presents, a daughter.

JERRY LEWIS

$\mathcal{M}$y Dear Daughter: Be very good. Do not bump yourself. Do not eat matches. Do not play with scissors or cats. Do not forget your dad. Sleep when your mother wishes it. Love us both. Try to know how we love you. *That* you will never learn. Good-night and God keep you, and bless you.

Your Dad

RICHARD HARDING-DAVIS

$\mathcal{O}$f course there were areas of safety; nothing could get at me if I curled up on my father's lap, holding on to his ear with one thumb tucked into it. He had a big brown moustache and a wide Haldane nose with a small lump on it which I liked. When he kissed me it was rough and tickly. Across his front was a gold watch chain with a big tick-tock watch on the end. In my own children's time it also had a chocolate tree which flowered into silver-paper-covered chocolates. All about him was safe.

NAOMI MITCHISON

To an old father, nothing is more sweet than a daughter. Boys are more spirited, but their ways are not so tender.

EURIPIDES

A girl! She's my daughter! She's my pride.

father of
IRINI SPANIDOU

I always preferred the outdoor chores, and generally helped my father pick the fruit, feed the pigs, and gather the eggs. He was a kind, gentle man, my refuge whenever anything went wrong. He made me feel that I was very special.

ESTHER PETERSON

He wasn't one to always show his emotions, but he did the night he became a father. He was just beaming. Suddenly Arthur couldn't smile enough or even say enough.

BRYANT GUMBEL,
about Arthur Ashe

Is thy face like thy mother's, my fair child, Ada, sole daughter of my house and heart?

BYRON,
Childe Harold

$\mathcal{B}$ecause parents are the first models for everything, the parent of the opposite sex carries a special responsibility: the child's first guide to dealing with the opposite half of the human race is the crucial one. How carefully a little girl is taught by her father, and how thoroughly she learns his lessons, may well determine how she enjoys the rewards of bedroom and, for the women who reach it, boardroom.

SUZANNE FIELDS

$\mathcal{I}$ remember being at a point below his knees and looking up at the vast length of him. He was six foot three; his voice was big. He was devastatingly attractive—even to his daughter as a child.... His voice was so beautiful, so enveloping. He was just bigger and better than anyone else.

ANJELICA HUSTON,
about her father, John Huston

$\mathcal{A}$lmost every time I watch my daughters playing near me, especially in a physical way, an unusual feeling takes hold of me. I do not identify with the big smiling male whose offspring play at his feet, although I do expect to feel like this, looking at their tiny bodies and my own big one. On the contrary, I feel small and open. I feel as if the three of us are learning independently how to be dependent on one another.

MORDECHAI RIMOR

*A*rthur always had his arms around [his daughter] Camera. When he talked about her, his face would light up like stars in the sky. He showed more feeling for his daughter than I had seen him show his whole life. He wanted to see her take her First Communion and to see her finish high school and to give her away in marriage. He wanted to be there to see her do these things because his mother wasn't around to see him do them.

HORACE ASHE,
uncle of Arthur Ashe

*Y*our daddy's upstairs. You can call him *Mr. President* now.

MAUDE SHAW,
to Caroline Kennedy,
after her father's election

*Y*ou can touch them with your eyes.

PABLO PICASSO,
to his daughter Paloma,
warning her not to play with
his art materials

*A*fter the birth of his daughter in 1945, Mr. Hirschfeld began to indulge in *the harmless insanity,* as he says, of hiding her name at least once in each of his drawings.

GLENN COLLINS,
about the artist, Al Hirschfeld

15

My daughters see me as an integral part of their lives. They can come to me in happiness and sadness. I am involved in their discipline as well as their creativity and fun. We are able to learn and share together.

GERALD M. TUCKMAN

I'm not jealous of Margot [her sister], never have been. I don't envy her good looks or her beauty. It is only that I long for Daddy's real love: not only as his child, but for me—Anne, myself.

ANNE FRANK

And for all the dads—and granddads making up for lost time—who know the difference between heat rash and roseola, I hope your Father's Day necktie is a beauty. And that your sons grow up to be just like their daddies.

ANITA DIAMANT

It was a peculiar, mutual dependence that we had: I wanted *his* attention; he wanted *mine*. He believed that if I would only sit still and listen, he could hand me the world, whole and flawless, like a peeled pear on a silver plate. I didn't want to sit still, and I didn't want the peeled pear. I wanted to find life on my own, in my own way, to stumble upon it like a surprise in a field—the ruddy if misshapen apple that falls from an unpruned tree.

COLETTE DOWLING

$\mathcal{F}$aced with the hypothetical situation of a daughter throwing a tantrum in a shopping mall and demanding a toy, only a minute fraction [of today's fathers] gave the sucker answers: *Get her what she wants,* and, *Bribe her with something else.* A small minority, bringing the ethics of business into the family, would lie their way out of it: *Tell her you don't have enough money.* But most dads say they would *sit her down and talk with her until she calms down,* proving that, if nothing else, this generation of fathers reads parenting books.

JERRY ADLER

17

*J*ust what is it that fathers do?
Love you. They kiss you and hug you when you need them.
What would you like to do with your dad?
I'd want him to talk to me.

Nancy R. Gibbs,
*interview with Megan, age eight,
on her absentee father*

*M*artha was trained from a young age to watch animals for the meaning behind their walking, nuzzling, snuffling, growling, and human beings for the counterparts of the same actions. She lived with this knowledge and these observed discoveries the whole of her life. I believe she owes this to her father. She once told me that Dr. Graham had said, *Bodies never lie.*

Agnes De Mille,
on the dancer, Martha Graham

I have not become the happy househusband finding great joy in his freedom…. But something else *is* happening. There is a very subtle change in my role that is more important and more rewarding than anything I anticipated. I am becoming the authority on the care of my daughter. I am making the daily decisions about her care, and my wife has begun to defer to my opinion. I am the primary care person. I am the expert. I am trusted…. My greatest reward is knowing that I do make a difference in the way my daughter is growing up.

John B. Ferguson

I was raised as my father's oldest son. I have always known how to fish, and I have always known how to talk back. I don't know if we girls who were so raised missed out on the standard romantic attachment to our fathers, or if it took a different form.

ANNA QUINDLEN

As the lily among thorns, so is my love among the daughters.

SONG OF SOLOMON 2:2

The only problems I had were with my own children, who sometimes grew jealous of my attentions to the show-kids. I remember that Marlo once was furious because I sang *her* song, *Daddy's Little Girl*, to Sherry.

DANNY THOMAS

But, Daddy, I can't! And he replied with those words that have stayed with me these many years: *There's no such word as "can't."*…If my father said something was so, then that's the way it was, but how could there not be such a word as *can't* if I could hear and see and say it?—though eventually I realized it was another way of saying, *Never give up.*

SUSAN KENNEY

I could stand on my hands. I could walk on my hands. I could stand-bend *backwards* and touch the floor with my hands and then walk in this position hands and feet. I could turn handsprings. I could do a flying somersault off Dad's shoulders. Off a diving board I could do a one-and-a-half. I could do a half gainer…. It was very exciting to be able to do all these things. We had great fun and a real sense of accomplishment as small kids. Thank you, Dad.

KATHARINE HEPBURN

$\mathcal{M}$y father encouraged my interests in science and art, but he never forgot to tell me that he thought I was beautiful, too.

SUZANNE FIELDS,
from a case study

$\mathcal{I}$n the middle of the Grand Canyon we found the ugliest dog you'd ever seen—someone had abandoned it four days earlier, and it had been starving. My father handed it to me, and I held this dog in my arms and calmed it down and grew to love it tremendously. After the trip it was in the newspapers that we had found this dog—we named her Rocky—and the owner came and took her away from me. I remember just crying and crying and feeling horrendous heartbreak. Then on the day we were flying home, we were all in this airplane, and my father was late. He finally came with this big cardboard box and walked straight over to me. In the box was a big straw hat. I lifted it up, and there was my dog. He had somehow saved the day and brought this animal back to me. I suddenly had an understanding of this overwhelming love he had for me. I felt I was somebody tremendously special that he could have done something magical for me.

KERRY KENNEDY CUOMO,
about her father, Robert F. Kennedy

$\mathcal{W}$ell, you both work where you live. I'm going to school.

CHELSEA CLINTON,
*to her parents on Take Our
Daughters to Work Day*

Frequently, fathers seem to be seeking in a firstborn daughter the comradeship they can't have with their wives because their wives are always starting dinner…. While their wives were definitely expected to be noncompetitive and nonachieving, the men took pride in a competitively successful daughter. She was often the favorite because she, unlike a son, could reflect well on her father without becoming a rival.

GAIL SHEEHY,
Passages

Father was a perfectionist. We had to hop to everything and have marvelous table manners. I could only wear navy blue and gray and white. He wanted me to be interested in tennis and horses just like a little princess, but I couldn't stand such things.

RAQUEL WELCH

You teach your daughters the diameters of the planets, and wonder when you have done that they do not delight in your company.

SAMUEL JOHNSON

I have never had any person in my life I love as much as my daughter. And I would trade nothing for her.

FRED DEAN

You've got to go to school, he would say, *and I'm not sending you to play either…. Remember, only the strong people survive in this world. God gave you a brain: use it….* He and I talked more than he did with the other girls.

SHIRLEY CHISHOLM

With my father life became an adventure. The minute he walked in the door at night, even the house seemed to take on a new energy, like a surge of electricity. Everything became charged, brighter, more colorful, more exciting…. All fathers are, at first, heroes to their daughters, even when they're anything but heroic.

VICTORIA SECUNDA

I think one of the things that has made Chelsea's life bearable as an only child is that we have done so many things together. I have driven her to school every day since kindergarten, unless I was away. The morning is our time.

PRESIDENT BILL CLINTON

GOOD
GIRL–BAD
GIRL

⌖   She is moody, vulnerable,
     rebellious, sexual.

⌖   He is cautious, demanding,
     protective, supportive.

I was in awe of my father. As a girl I would do naughty things just to gain his attention.

JANE FONDA

*F*ather, chancing to chastise
His indignant daughter Sue,
Said: *I hope you realize*
That this hurts me more than you.

Susan straightway ceased to roar;
If that's really true, said she,
I can stand a good deal more;
Pray go on, and don't mind me.

HARRY GRAHAM,
Ruthless Rhymes, 1899

*R*aising kids is part joy and part guerilla warfare.

ED ASNER

I thought what a bad daughter I was, that I'd been more like a stranger than a daughter to him and had never been a help to this lonely spirit, this sick old man when he was left all alone on his Olympus. Yet he was, after all, my father, a father who had done his best to love me and to whom I owed good things as well as bad—more good than bad, in fact.

SVETLANA ALILUYEVA (STALIN),
on her father's death

Sometimes when I look at my lovely grown-up daughter, I also see the adorable tow-headed child she was at three. But who, I wonder, was that strange teenager I hardly knew who came between the two?

GENE KOHN

As a teenager, I hated my father's taste in everything from food to fashion. Now I find, with feelings of both horror and delight, that I love the food he eats and adore the clothes he wears.

LAURA STEVENS PARKER

At the moment that a boy of thirteen is turning towards girls, a girl of thirteen is turning on her mother. This girl can get rather unreasonable, often saying such comical things as, *Listen, this is my life!*

BILL COSBY

My daughter's teenage years have been a time of mood swings. One day I'm flying high and the next day I'm down in the dumps!

NICK BEILENSON

My father taught me to be independent and cocky, and free-thinking, but he could not stand it if I disagreed with him.

SARA MAITLAND

My father was the most important influence in my life. He made me believe that I could achieve anything if I worked hard enough. And he made me feel terribly attractive. Whenever I'd worry about ever getting a boyfriend, he'd laugh and say, *Are you kidding? I'll have to beat off the guys with a stick. You'll see.* His whole approach was to make me feel good about myself, and most of the time he succeeded. I think if fathers do nothing else, that's a great thing.

VICTORIA SECUNDA,
quoting Harriet, forty, in a case study

A man can deceive his fiancée or his mistress as much as he likes, and, in the eyes of a woman he loves, an ass may pass for a philosopher; but a daughter is a different matter.

ANTON CHEKHOV

There's nothing wrong with a teenage girl that reasoning with her won't aggravate.

ANONYMOUS

It was an indescribable feeling to see my daughter, self-possessed and self-confident, as she mounted the stage to receive her high school diploma. Could it have been only four years ago that she was an awkward, moody, uncertain beanpole of a kid?

ROGER NICHOLS

Having an overprotective father at fourteen was embarrassing, but having one at twenty-one is too much.

JENNIFER CONCEPCION

I was enormously close to my father…I imagine we were treated the way boys are treated. Dad insisted on discussing politics and world affairs at the dinner table. He wanted us to think, weigh facts, form opinions. He had more of an impact on preparing me for the outside world than my mother.

DR. JOYCE BROTHERS

Romeo looks more like Ratso to me.

CHUCK LEWIS,
upon meeting his sixteen-year-old daughter's first love

Why is it that when you can finally afford to buy your teenage daughter clothing fit for a princess, she seems to make a concerted effort to look more like a pauper?

NAT RICHMOND

FATHER OF THE BRIDE

❧ She is in love with another man; she is moving on.

❧ He feels proud, vulnerable, old.

*Y*ou're not really getting married, are you?

Dad, stop that!

FATHER AND DAUGHTER

*A*n undutiful Daughter will prove an
unmanageable Wife.

BENJAMIN FRANKLIN

$\mathcal{I}$ was so proud of you and thrilled at having you so close to me on our long walk in Westminster Abbey, but when I handed your hand to the Archbishop I felt I had lost something very precious.... I have watched you grow up all these years with pride under the skilful direction of Mummy, who as you know is the most marvellous person in the World in my eyes, and I can, I know, always count on you, and now Philip, to help us in our work. Your leaving us has left a great blank in our lives but do remember that your old home is still yours and do come back to it as much and as often as possible. I can see that you are sublimely happy with Philip which is right but don't forget us is the wish of

Your ever loving & devoted
Papa

KING GEORGE VI,
to Princess Elizabeth

$\mathcal{M}$ay God forgive girls for making parents and grandparents old before their time.

NAGUIB MAHFOUZ,
The Cairo Trilogy

$\mathcal{M}$ay our Lord guide your steps and grant you success and peace of mind. I cannot give you any better advice than to imitate your mother in every respect, both great and small.

NAGUIB MAHFOUZ,
The Cairo Trilogy

*T*wenty years ago, all a father was expected to do was support his daughter financially—until another man could support her. Now, he has to encourage independence, helping to create an attitude that will allow her to succeed in her own right.

JOAN MINNINGER

I know your disposition, Lizzy. I know that you could be neither happy nor respectable, unless you truly esteemed your husband; unless you looked up to him as a superior. Your lively talents would place you in the greatest danger in an unequal marriage. You could scarcely escape discredit and misery. My child, let me not have the grief of seeing *you* unable to respect your partner in life.

JANE AUSTEN,
Pride and Prejudice

*I*f you get into any trouble, don't forget that you can always call me at the office.

ALAN ALDA,
to his daughter's college class

*Y*ou fathers will understand…she gets a little older and you quit worrying about her meeting the wrong guy. You worry about her meeting the *right* guy, and that's the biggest fear of all because you lose her.

Father of the Bride, Screenplay by
FRANCINE GOODRICH, ALBERT HACKETT,
NANCY MEYERS, AND CHARLES SHYER

$\mathcal{I}$ only told her to have a happy life.

HISASHI OWADA,
father of Masako, on day of her
wedding to Crown Prince Naruhito

I AM
MY
FATHER'S
DAUGHTER

><->-o-<->-<

☞ She is strong, independent, competent.

☞ He is proud.

$\mathcal{I}$ guess that's one of the reasons Daddy and I are so much alike. You do not have to be of the same gender to be a chip off the old block.

BARBARA MANDRELL

$\mathcal{H}$e brought me up to believe all the things I do believe, and they're the values on which I fought the election. It's passionately interesting to me that the things I learned in a small town, in a very modest home, are just the things that I believe have won the election…I owe almost everything to my father.

MARGARET THATCHER

*H*er way of handling any problem was to say, *Now what would my father have done?* and she'd sit with her head in her hands thinking it out until she came up with an answer. She didn't love her father—she *idolized* him. He was the one great love in her life. No other man ever measured up to him.

MARY S. LOVELL,
about Beryl Markham

*M*y father's a little like this. I think I got it from him. He would say things like *Trust everyone, Shel—but cut the cards.*

MICHELLE PFEIFFER

*Y*ou appear to me so superior, so elevated above other men; I contemplate you with such strange mixture of humility, admiration, reverence, love and pride, that very little superstition would be necessary to make me worship you as a superior being…I had rather not live than not be the daughter of such a man.

THEODOSIA BURR,
daughter of Aaron Burr

*I*t's only when you grow up, and step back from him, or leave him for your own career and your own home—it's only then that you can measure his greatness and fully appreciate it. Pride reinforces love.

MARGARET TRUMAN

$\mathcal{B}$ut he gave me the basic tools, and it wasn't fancy philosophical stuff. He used to say all the time, *I will always love you but I won't always like what you do.* And, you know, as a child I would come up with 900 hypotheses. It would always end with something like, *Well, you mean, if I murdered somebody and was in jail and you came to see me, you would still love me?* And he would say: *Absolutely! I will always love you, but I would be deeply disappointed and I would not like what you did because it would have been wrong.*

HILLARY RODHAM CLINTON,
about her father, Hugh Rodham

Sara, why didn't Daddy teach us about money?

WENDY WASSERSTEIN,
The Sisters Rosensweig

He dominated my life as long as he lived, and was the love of my life for many years after he died.

ELEANOR ROOSEVELT,
about her father

I think I'd like to fly, I told the family casually that evening, knowing full well I'd die if I didn't. *Not a bad idea,* said my father equally casually. *When do you start?*

AMELIA EARHART

It took her forty years of living on the same earth to say no to her father. She brought her fist down on the dining room table and shouted one night, *Who do you think you are, God? Yes,* her celebrated father replied. *Well, you're not,* she said, and the great man's magical powers over her were broken.

GAIL SHEEHY,
Passages

It is well known that there are many women who have a strong attachment to their father; nor need they be in any way neurotic.

SIGMUND FREUD

I don't think I'm the best singer or the best musician in country music, but I am very proud of being so versatile. When I run around the stage, going from instrument to instrument, what you see is Daddy's confidence in me.

BARBARA MANDRELL

This is the Ronald Reagan America will remember, I told myself then—serious and persuasive one moment, playful and energetic the next, proud enough of himself and his country that he can stand before a national political convention and play with balloons. That's my father.

MAUREEN REAGAN

At the end, I said [the line] *I want to be your friend,* and I'll never forget it, because my dad was never very emotional—he didn't cry on camera or on stage. I touched him. I waited until his last close-up and he didn't expect it, and I touched him and I could see the tears well up in his eyes.

JANE FONDA

My plebe autobiography in progress has not encompassed him yet. He's in the works, though, and I've long considered him essential to understanding myself.

JILL JOHNSTON,
about her father

$\mathcal{I}$ felt bad about not knowing what to get him year after year. It was like admitting I didn't know him well enough to buy something that would make him happy. Throughout the year, I'd be on *gift alert.* Every time he said he liked something, I made a mental note.... He died three years ago.... Why didn't I know that what was in the boxes each Father's Day was unimportant? I was there to give them. That's all he really wanted.

ERMA BOMBECK

$\mathcal{S}$ervice is the rent we pay for living.

MARIAN WRIGHT EDELMAN,
lesson taught by her father

$\mathcal{I}$t is silly of me, a middle-aged woman, to call my dead father Daddy. It's not as if I were some giddy heiress anticipating the next installment of my allowance or Little Orphan Annie learning to get what she wants out of Daddy Warbucks, or yet some southern belle refusing to be her age.... I always called him Daddy.

GERMAINE GREER

$\mathcal{I}$n recent months Mr. Molinari has weighed a run for governor. But if his daughter wanted to run, he said, he would defer. *There are things about her that would make her the better candidate,* he said. *She is younger, she is a woman, she's pro-choice.*

CATHERINE S. MANEGOLD,
about Guy V. Molinari

*A*gain it hit me: First Father, First Daughter…. The President. My father. The President's daughter. Me.

MAUREEN REAGAN

*M*argaret [Sanger] always harbored a distinct ambivalence toward her father's political beliefs. On the one hand, she admired his convictions deeply and identified his radicalism as *the spring* from which she drank. She often quoted his admonition that the only obligation of his children was to *leave the world a better place*, but the emotional price of this iconoclasm also left a strong imprint.

ELLEN CHESSLER

*T*hen farewell, my dear; my loved
          daughter, adieu;
The last pang of life is in parting from
          you.

THOMAS JEFFERSON

I was left then with the dilemma of overcoming my father's criticisms and viewing him as a rehearsal for the tough world out there, or succumbing to the proposition that indeed I didn't have any talent and shouldn't even try. Either choice was a guarantee that stepping onto a stage would cause me profound anxiety. So *why* do it? Was it for audience approval? No, it was really a plea for my father's love.

SHIRLEY MACLAINE

41

Margaret Mead's father once told her, *It's a pity you aren't a boy; you'd have gone far.* By never allowing him too much power over her, she went literally to the ends of the earth.

GAIL SHEEHY

Unconsciously, I created a career for myself not unlike my father's. When I started lecturing, I found myself surrounded by people burdened with serious problems…and the moral as well as professional imperative was that I be the strong one and hold other people up. I am what is called a father's daughter.

MARIANNE WILLIAMSON

I was the only sibling who paid attention at the dinner table when the business was discussed and who worked at Lebenthal during the summers.

ALEXANDRA LEBENTHAL,
daughter of Jim Lebenthal

My father would come home and say, *You did well, but could you do better? It's hard out there.* Encouragement was tempered with realism.

HILLARY RODHAM CLINTON

I know I have my father wrapped around my finger, but he has me wrapped around his.

HOLLY HESTON

$\mathcal{B}$estowing pleasure upon a beloved father is much easier than discovering the joys of solitary achievements. It was easy for me to please my father; and this ease bred in me a desire to please men—a desire for the rewards of a good girl. They are by no means inconsiderable: safety and approval, the warm, incomparable atmosphere created when one pleases a man who has vowed, in his turn, to keep the wolf from the door.

MARY GORDON

$\mathcal{T}$he most important thing about our time together was this: whatever his politics or view of the role of women, he never made me think there was anything I couldn't do.

SUSAN KENNEY

$\mathcal{M}$arlo...was the first to attend U.S.C.... On the day we came home from her commencement, Marlo steered me into my office at home. She threw her diplomas down on my desk and said, *This is for* you. *Now, how do I become an actress?* What's a father to do? I told her that if it's what she really wanted, I'd do all I could to give her the proper advice.

DANNY THOMAS

$\mathcal{M}$y father always wanted to be the corpse at every funeral, the bride at every wedding and the baby at every christening.

ALICE ROOSEVELT LONGWORTH,
about her father, Theodore Roosevelt

$\mathcal{B}$ecause Daddy was a writer, I thought I wanted to be a writer when I was about twelve or thirteen. Then I decided that I was no good as a writer and that I definitely didn't want to be a writer. It was the last thing I wanted to be. So, when I graduated from Brown I got a job as an English teacher, because I didn't want to be a writer. Then I got married because I didn't want to be a writer. Then I learned to cook because I didn't want to be a writer...I got a job as a reporter on *The Tarrytown Daily News....* Of course the minute I started I just loved it.... But I still didn't want to be a writer.

SUSAN CHEEVER

$\mathcal{S}$he once told *McCall's* magazine that her father had *absolutely no career drive. I can't account for that. He was an enigma to me. I won't say cold, but reserved. It's only in the last ten years that we've learned to express affection openly. I think that a lot of my career drive is based on a childhood need to get Daddy's approval and attention.* Even as an adult, she still carried that need with her. It influenced her choice of men.

JASON BONDEROFF,
about Mary Tyler Moore

$\mathcal{W}$hy do I demand that he be gallant and brave? I don't demand that my mother be gallant and brave, do I? But yes, I do. I want both of them to be tough, dinky-di, reliable, stalwart, straight.

GERMAINE GREER

44

*D*ear Kath,

Can't let your twenty-first birthday go by without a wee bit of sentimental indulgence. You are now a free lance and your dad has no control over you. Just think of that! Doesn't it make you shudder when you think of the past twenty-one years of servitude. Just for that I now shall order you around as successfully in the future as in the past.

First, don't take life or its happenings too seriously. Lift up the corners of that mouth that I gave you one moonlit night.

Second, try to do one thing well—utilizing the experience of all preceding life and your own wit.

Third, never let yourself *hate* any person. It is the most devastating weapon of one's enemies.

Fourth, always remember that your dad is liable to call you all sorts of names when he disapproves of your behavior, but don't take him too seriously, and always come to him—whatever your difficulty—he may be able to help you. Impossibly, he may not be as stupid as he looks.

Fifth, forget all the above and remember only that I would love to kiss you twenty-one times and give you a million dollars—

Your hopeless Dad

LETTER TO KATHARINE HEPBURN

*M*ale friends, lovers and bosses should be people who look at you with respect and see your good qualities, the way a good father would.

JANE MYERS DREW

$\mathcal{I}$ had a terrific father. Don't get me wrong—my mother was also loving. But it's my dad who made me believe in myself. I remember my mom once telling me, *Don't act too smart—the boys won't like you.* To which my father responded, *Hogwash—she'll get smarter boys.*

VICTORIA SECUNDA,
quoting Adrienne, forty-two, in a case study

$\mathcal{C}$hanging my name meant defining myself as an adult, choosing my own label. Taking a new name was about growing up. It was about how, much as I loved him, I stopped being Daddy's little girl…. As long as I bore his name, some part of me was always Bill Flynn's girl, a sixth grader with scabby knees, a teenager whose hair curled on alternate sides, a writer who might or might not be as good as her dad…. Looking back, I'm glad that I chose names when I married. It pulled some doors closed and blew others open. I needed to be something other than a newsman's daughter who wanted to be just as good as her old man. As an adult woman, I am responsible for my own life and label. My name is what I say it is: My choice. Me.

SUSAN FERRARO

$\mathcal{M}$y father's words, too, come back to me in my work for human rights: *Each time a man stands up for an ideal or acts to improve the lot of others or strikes out against injustice, he sends forth a tiny ripple of hope, and crossing each other from a million different centers of energy and daring, those ripples build a current that can sweep down the mightiest walls of oppression and resistance.*

KERRY KENNEDY CUOMO

When he was alive, he created so much centrifugal force that it was hard to participate without getting swallowed up. The sun was just too bright. But in the afterglow, it is a little easier to breathe it in.

JAMIE BERNSTEIN

The very words *my father* always make me smile.

ANGELA CARTER

My father is just a mountain to me now, a man and not a mirror. This enables me to love him as I never could when I saw only my own splayed reflection in the lenses of his glasses. His expectations were hard on me, but they took me places I would never have gone otherwise.

ANNA QUINDLEN

Babe, pay no attention to what other people think. Just be yourself.

LILY TOMLIN'S FATHER,
advice to her

I was my father's daughter.... He is dead now and I am a grown woman and still I am my father's daughter.... I am many things besides, but I am daddy's girl too and so I will remain—all the way to the old folks' home.

PAULA WEIDEGER

Acknowledgments

Photograph on Title Page is reproduced with the permission of Laurie Parkinson.

Photograph on Contents Page is reproduced with the permission of Carol Cioppa.

Photograph on page 4 is reproduced with the permission of Marcia Joy Photographic.

Photograph on page 9 is reproduced with the permission of Evelyn Beilenson.

Photograph on page 12 is reproduced with the permission of Maureen and Keith Turkel.

Photograph on page 17 is reproduced with the permission of Esther and Laurence Beilenson.

Photograph on page 19 is reproduced with the permission of Phyllis and Rodney Alston, Sr.

Photograph on page 30 is reproduced with the permission of Barbara Kohn.

Photograph on page 33 is reproduced with the permission of Tracy Kay.

Photograph on page 35 is reproduced with the permission of Gloria Goldstein.

Photograph on page 37 is reproduced with the permission of Beth Jaykus.

Photograph on page 48 is reproduced with the permission of Nick Beilenson.